WEIRD-BUT-TRUE FACTS ABOUT INVENTIONS

BY ARNOLD RINGSTAD • ILLUSTRATED BY KATHLEEN PETELINSEK

Published by The Child's World®
1980 Lookout Drive • Mankato, MN 56003-1705
800-599-READ • www.childsworld.com

Acknowledgments
The Child's World®: Mary Berendes, Publishing Director
Red Line Editorial: Editorial direction
The Design Lab: Design
Amnet: Production

ISBN 9781614734154
LCCN 2012946522

Printed in the United States of America
Mankato, MN
October, 2013
PA02204

About the Author

Arnold Ringstad lives in Minneapolis, Minnesota. He has a Nikola Tesla T-shirt.

About the Illustrator

Kathleen Petelinsek loves to draw and paint. She lives next to a lake in southern Minnesota with her husband, Dale; two daughters, Leah and Anna; two dogs, Gary and Rex; and her fluffy cat, Emma.

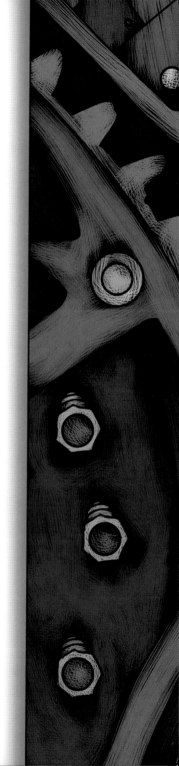

TABLE OF CONTENTS

INTRODUCTION

From ancient vending machines to cars that drive themselves, people have always been inventing the future. Inventions do everything from fastening your clothes to storing millions of megabytes of data. They have been created after years of hard work or stumbled upon simply by accident. Get ready to learn some strange facts about inventions—and remember, they are all true!

ANCIENT INVENTIONS

A Byzantine inventor created the flamethrower.

The weapon was known as Greek fire. It was used in sea battles. The process for making Greek fire was kept secret, and it eventually was lost. No one today knows for sure how to make it.

The first vending machine was invented in approximately 100 AD.

The inventor, Heron, lived in Alexandria, Egypt. People put a coin into the machine and holy water came out.

The first steam engine was only used as a toy.

Heron of Alexandria invented it. The engine used steam power to make a metal ball spin around. Useful steam engines were not made until approximately 1,600 years later.

The Ancient Egyptians invented the first toothpaste, breath mints, and eye makeup.

People living in Finland invented ice skates more than 5,000 years ago.

They used sharpened animal bones as blades rather than metal blades.

Ancient Egyptians used water clocks to tell time.

These clocks dripped water at a steady rate. They were used as early as 1500 BC. They were the most accurate clocks available for more than 3,000 years.

The compass was invented about 2,000 years ago in China.

It was not used for **navigation** at first. Instead, it was likely used to help design cities, so buildings would face certain directions.

The ancient Greek inventor Archimedes invented a machine to lift enemy boats out of the water and drop them down again to smash them.

Archimedes lived between 287 and 212 BC.

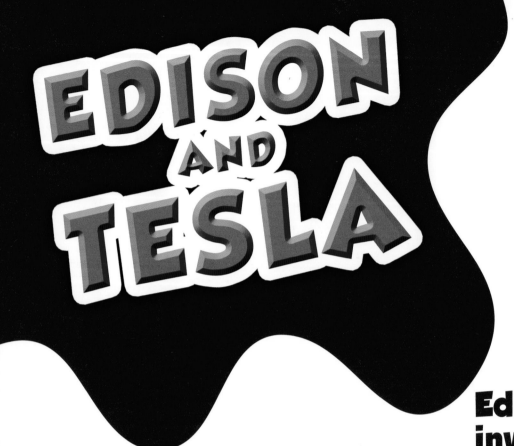

EDISON AND TESLA

Thomas Edison (1847–1931) received more than 1,000 patents for his inventions.

He also filed between 500 and 600 unsuccessful applications. That is about one patent every two weeks during his career.

Edison tried to invent a machine to talk to the dead.

Edison was responsible for the electric chair.

Edison had a rivalry with inventor Nikola Tesla (1856–1943) over whose type of electricity was best. Edison preferred direct current (DC), while Tesla preferred alternating current (AC). Edison created the electric chair using AC. He wanted to show that Tesla's type of electricity was too dangerous to use. AC was actually better, and it is still used in homes today.

Tesla claimed to invent an electric death ray that could be used by the military.

He claimed it could shoot down 10,000 airplanes from 250 miles (400 km) away. However, he could not find enough money to fund his experiments so he never tried to build it.

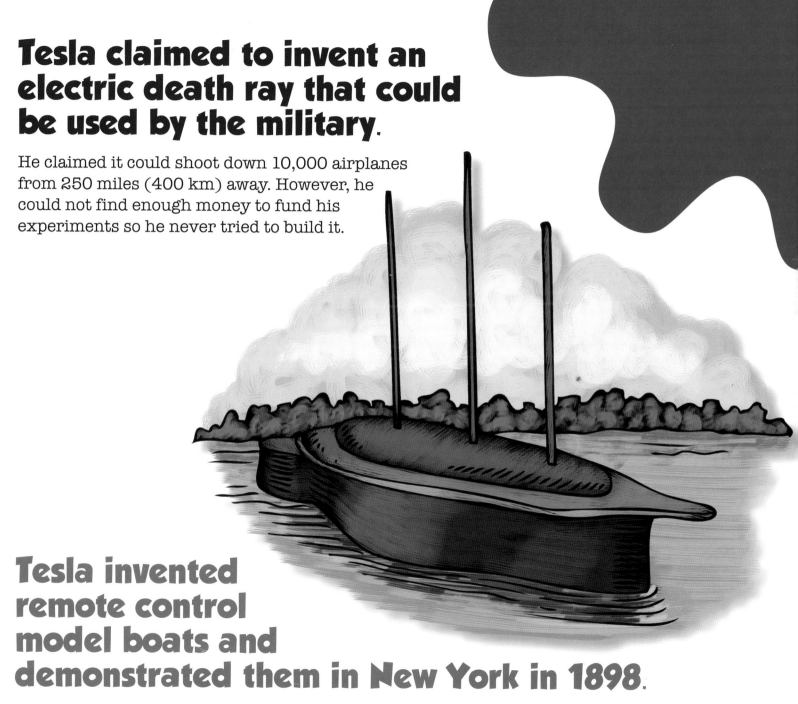

Tesla invented remote control model boats and demonstrated them in New York in 1898.

Edison invented an electric vote recorder to help Congress work faster, but they didn't want to use it.

In 1890, Edison invented the first talking doll.

It had a tiny **record player** inside of it. Approximately 500 were sold, but customers returned most of them. The dolls were fragile and broke easily.

Edison had plans to make concrete houses and concrete furniture.

People felt they were too ugly, and they never caught on.

Tesla invented the radio, but another inventor named Guglielmo Marconi took credit for it.

When asked about it, Tesla said, "Marconi is a good fellow. Let him continue. He is using 17 of my patents." Tesla didn't receive credit for the invention until a few months after his own death.

TECHNOLOGY FIRSTS

The first TV remote control, made in 1950, was connected to the television by a wire.

The first wireless model came out five years later.

The first cell phone was more than a foot long (30 cm).

It weighed almost 2 pounds (1 kg). It came out in 1983 and cost approximately $4,000. By 2012, cell phones weighed less than .5 pounds (.2 kg). Many cost under $50.

The first hard disk drive cost tens of thousands of dollars.

It held 5 megabytes of information and weighed approximately 2,000 pounds (900 kg). Today's hard drives cost at least 100 million times less per megabyte. They hold more than 1 million times more information and weigh 10,000 times less.

The first camera was invented in the 1820s.

However, it took eight hours to take a single picture.

The Wright Brothers' first airplane flight in 1903 traveled 120 feet (37 m).

This is less than half the wingspan of the largest jet airliners flying today. The plane had a top speed of approximately 30 miles per hour (50 km/h).

The first MP3 player could hold 32 megabytes of music, which is five to ten songs.

It was released in 1998. By 2012, MP3 players could hold more than 40,000 songs.

The first robotic pet was the AIBO dog.

Sony Corporation started selling the AIBO in 1999. The robots cost up to $2,000.

The first U.S. space probe, *Explorer 1*, weighed approximately 30 pounds (14 kg).

It was launched in 1958. The *Galileo* space probe, launched almost 30 years later, weighed approximately 5,200 pounds (2,360 kg).

The first television was invented in 1923.

One of the inventors called it a televisor. Other suggested names for it were radiovision, audiovision, and farscope.

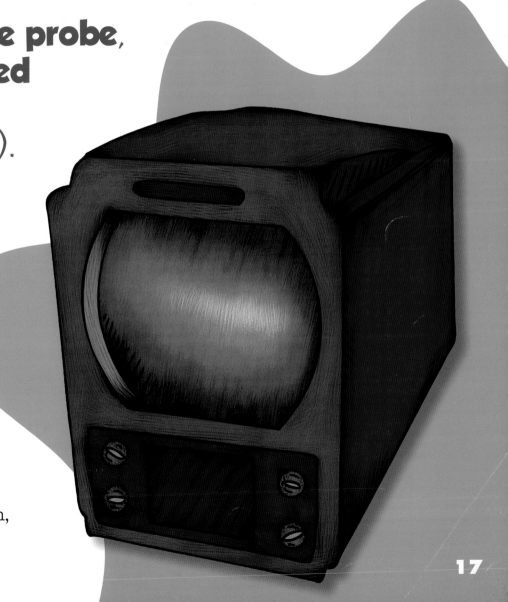

TRANSPORTATION INNOVATIONS

In 2012, companies were working to invent cars that can drive themselves.

One company's cars received driver's licenses for them to operate in the state of Nevada. However, a human being had to be in the car to drive in an emergency.

The first train moved at less than 5 miles per hour (8 km/h).

It was first demonstrated in 1804. Today's fastest trains can travel more than 300 miles per hour (480 km/h).

The Italian inventor Leonardo da Vinci drew plans for a glider and a parachute in the 1400s.

People finally built and tested his parachute in 2000 and his glider in 2002. They both worked.

The first hot air balloon that could carry people was invented in France in 1783.

A balloon was used during the battle of Fleurus between France and Great Britain 11 years later in 1794. It served as an observation post.

The first jet aircraft flew in 1939 at a top speed of 435 miles per hour (700 km/h).

The fastest jet aircraft in 2012, the SR-71 Blackbird, can fly at nearly 2,200 miles per hour (3,300 km/h).

Many of the earliest cars were electric cars.

William Morrison of Iowa invented an electric car in 1891. Gasoline-powered cars did not become popular until after 1908, when Henry Ford introduced his famous Model T car.

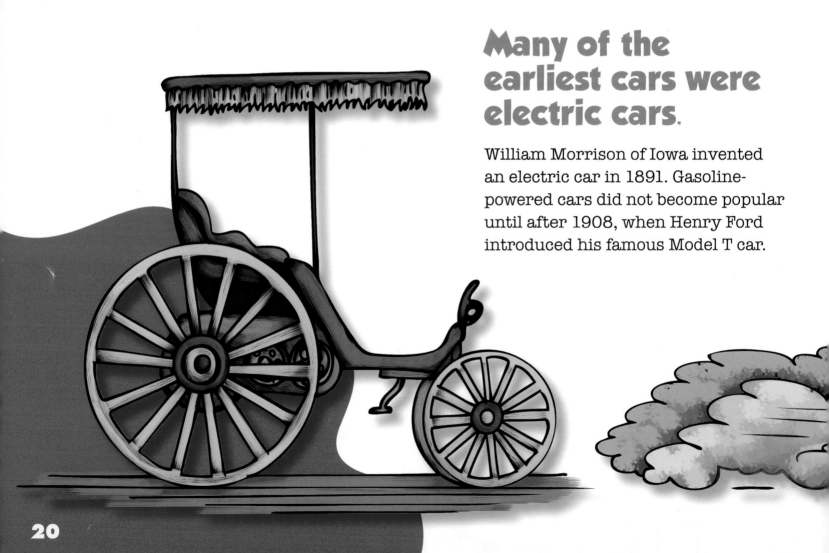

The fastest vehicle ever was the *Helios 2* spacecraft.

It traveled more than 150,000 miles per hour (250,000 km/h) in 1976. *Helios 2* was designed to fly close to the sun in order to study it.

The land speed record is 763 miles per hour (1,228 km/h).

It was set by a jet-powered car in 1997. The jet engines were the same kind found on some fighter jets.

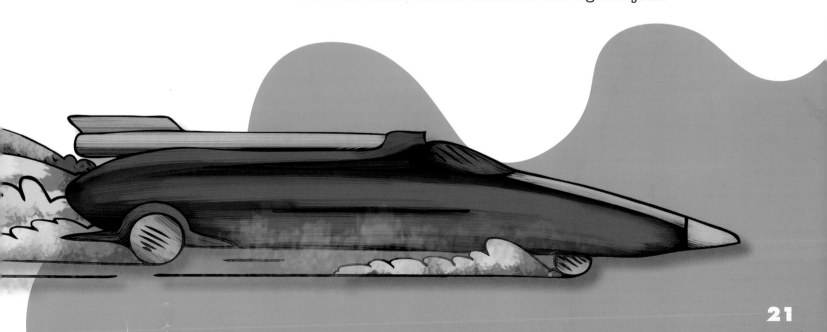

MORE WEIRD INVENTION FACTS

A melted candy bar resulted in the invention of the microwave oven.

The inventor was standing near a machine called a **magnetron** when the chocolate bar in his pocket melted. He realized the microwaves from the machine caused things to heat up.

The first microwave oven weighed more than 750 pounds (340 kg) and cost almost $5,000.

The inventor of the Celsius temperature scale originally made his scale backwards.

Anders Celsius set 100 degrees Celsius as the freezing point of water. Zero degrees Celsius was the boiling point. They were switched after his death in 1744.

More than 30 people tried to patent their own dishwashing machine design between 1870 and 1895.

Josephine Cochrane of Illinois invented the first popular dishwasher in 1886. Her company became KitchenAid, one of the major appliance makers of the 1900s.

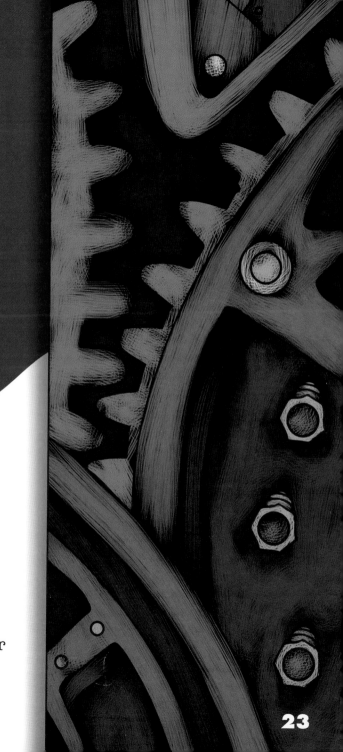

Canned food was invented in 1810, but household can openers were not invented until 1870.

Until the opener was invented, canned food was mostly used by soldiers. They usually used a hammer and chisel to open the cans.

Albert Einstein predicted the invention of the laser.

In 1916, he said building one was possible. The first working laser was not made until 1960.

The composer Ludwig van Beethoven's music helped invent compact discs (CDs).

CDs were originally going to hold about an hour of music. They were made with a larger capacity so they could hold Beethoven's entire Ninth Symphony—more than 70 minutes—on one disc.

The inventor of the shopping cart hired fake shoppers to push the carts around his store.

He did so to make the carts seem popular and encourage others to use them.

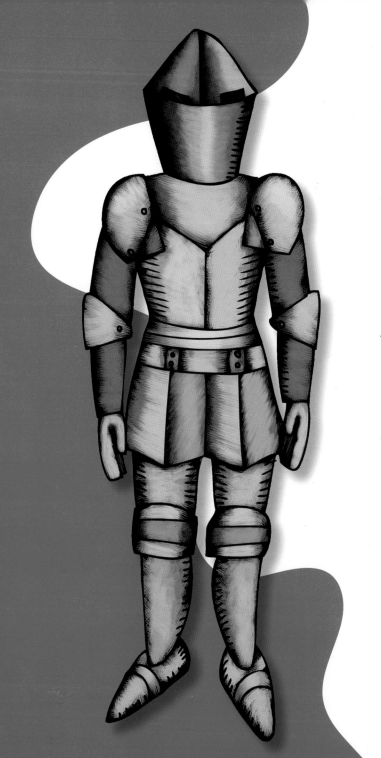

Leonardo da Vinci designed a robotic knight around 1495.

A modern scientist was inspired by da Vinci's designs. He was designing space robots for NASA in the early 2000s.

A dog helped invent Velcro.

The inventor, George de Mestral, was on a hunting trip. He noticed that burrs from plants were stuck to his dog's fur. He looked at the burrs under a microscope and saw that tiny hooks made the burr stick to the fur. He used this idea to create Velcro.

Fortune cookies were not originally from China.

They were invented in San Francisco, California, in 1914 by Japanese restaurant owner Makoto Hagiwara.

Pinball machines, invented in 1931, were banned in New York City in late 1941.

Authorities considered it a form of gambling. The mayor personally smashed pinball machines in public.

Sliced bread was invented in 1928 in the United States.

By 1933, 80 percent of all bread sold in the country was sliced.

The first alarm clock was made in Germany in the 1300s.

The iron clock hung on the wall and a metal weight fell and hit a bronze bell when it was time for the alarm.

More than 4,000 inventors have patented their own mousetrap designs in the United States.

Vulcanized rubber was invented by accident.

Its inventor, Charles Goodyear, spilled a mixture of rubber and chemicals onto a hot stove. He noticed that the rubber hardened. Vulcanized rubber is used in car tires, shoes, and hockey pucks.

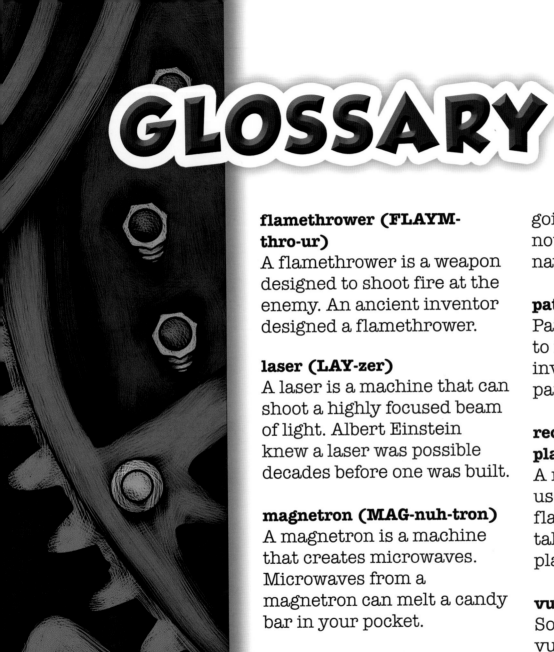

GLOSSARY

flamethrower (FLAYM-thro-ur)
A flamethrower is a weapon designed to shoot fire at the enemy. An ancient inventor designed a flamethrower.

laser (LAY-zer)
A laser is a machine that can shoot a highly focused beam of light. Albert Einstein knew a laser was possible decades before one was built.

magnetron (MAG-nuh-tron)
A magnetron is a machine that creates microwaves. Microwaves from a magnetron can melt a candy bar in your pocket.

navigation (nav-uh-GAY-shun)
Navigation is the act of figuring out where you are going. Chinese inventors did not use their compasses for navigation.

patents (PAT-ents)
Patents are legal rights to make money from an invention. Edison held many patents.

record player (REK-ord play-ur)
A record player is a machine used to listen to music on flat wax records. Edison's talking doll had a record player inside of it.

vulcanized (VUL-kan-eyesd)
Something that was vulcanized was made more durable with chemicals. Charles Goodyear created vulcanized rubber.

LEARN MORE

BOOKS

Harper, Charise Mericle. *Imaginative Inventions*. New York: Little, Brown, 2001.

Harrison, Ian. *The Book of Inventions*. Washington, DC: National Geographic Society, 2004.

Hopkins, Lee Bennett. *Incredible Inventions*. New York: Greenwillow, 2009.

WEB SITES

Visit our Web site for links about weird invention facts: **childsworld.com/links**

Note to Parents, Teachers, and Librarians: We routinely verify our Web links to make sure they are safe and active sites. So encourage your readers to check them out!

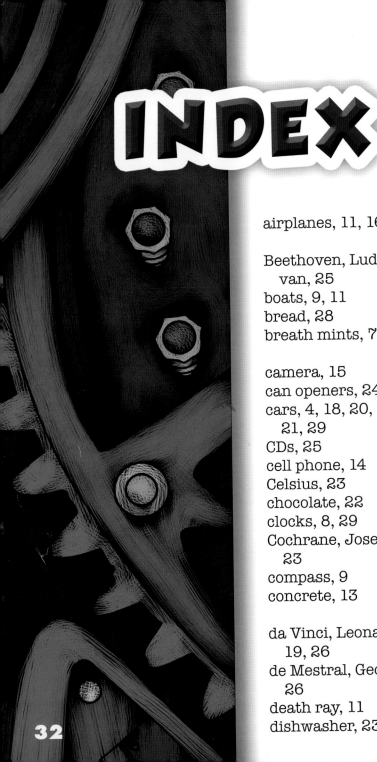

INDEX